classical chillout

for solo piano

classical chillout

for solo piano

Chester Music
London/New York/Paris/Sydney/Copenhagen/Berlin/Madrid/Tokyo

Published by
Chester Music
14–15 Berners Street, London W1T 3LJ, UK.

Exclusive Distributors:
Music Sales Limited
Distribution Centre, Newmarket Road, Bury St Edmunds, Suffolk IP33 3YB, UK.
Music Sales Pty Limited
20 Resolution Drive, Caringbah, NSW 2229, Australia.

Order No. CH64053
ISBN 0-7119-9237-1
This book © Copyright 2002 Chester Music Limited.

Cover design by Phil Gambrill.

Printed in the EU.

Your Guarantee of Quality:
As publishers, we strive to produce every book to the highest commercial standards.
This book has been carefully designed to minimise awkward page turns and to make
playing from it a real pleasure.
Particular care has been given to specifying acid-free, neutral-sized paper made from
pulps which have not been elemental chlorine bleached. This pulp is from farmed
sustainable forests and was produced with special regard for the environment.
Throughout, the printing and binding have been planned to ensure a sturdy, attractive
publication which should give years of enjoyment.
If your copy fails to meet our high standards, please inform us and we will gladly
replace it or offer a refund.

www.musicsales.com

ave verum corpus

in D major, K618

By Wolfgang Amadeus Mozart

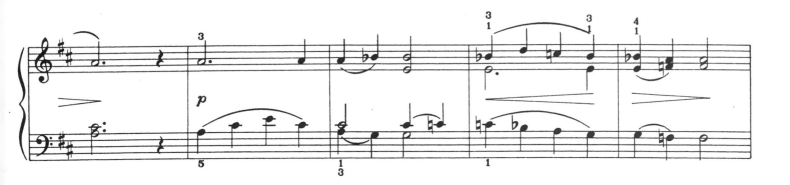

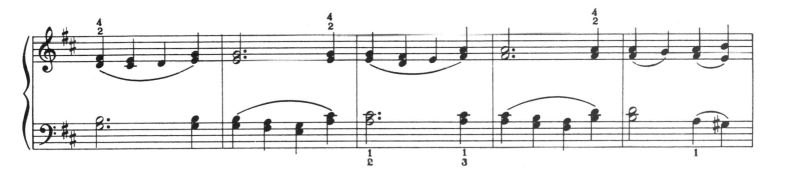

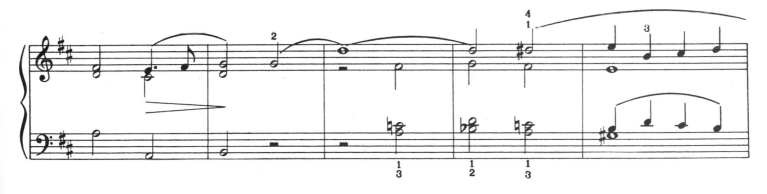

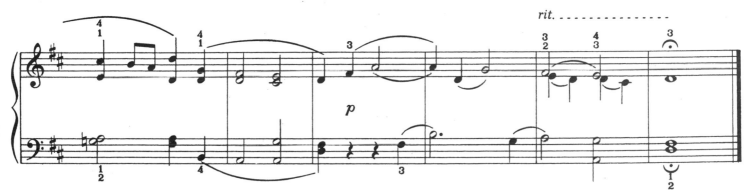

the ashokan farewell

(from the tv series "the civil war")

By Jay Ungar
Arranged by Jack Long

Freely, with expression

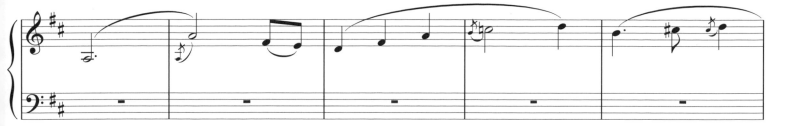

a tempo (but still a little freely) ♩ = *c.*88

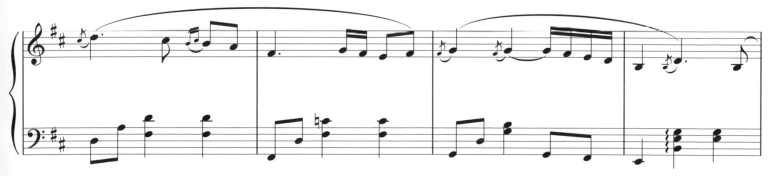

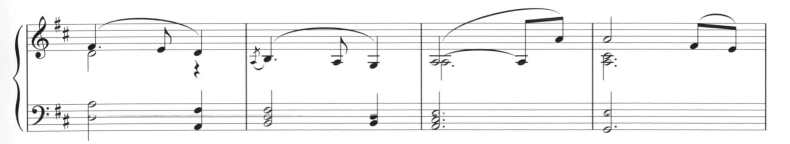

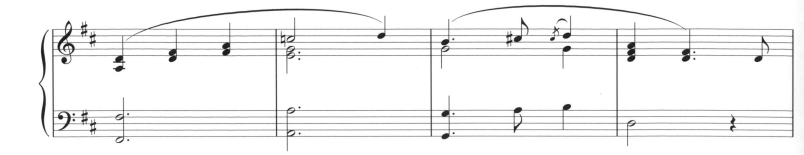

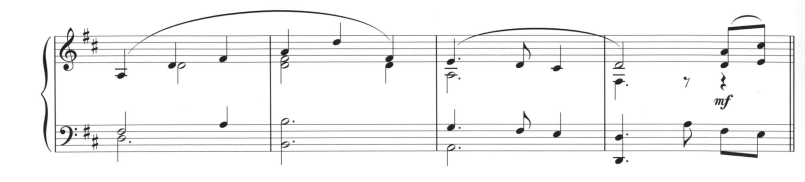

molto rit.　　　　　　　　a tempo

poco dim.

rall.

perpetuum mobile

By Simon Jeffes
Arranged by Jack Long

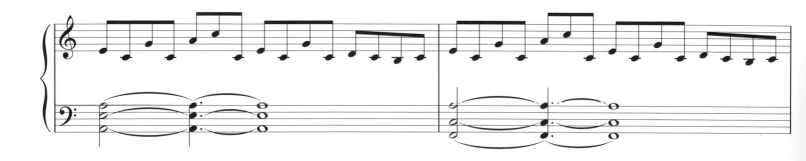

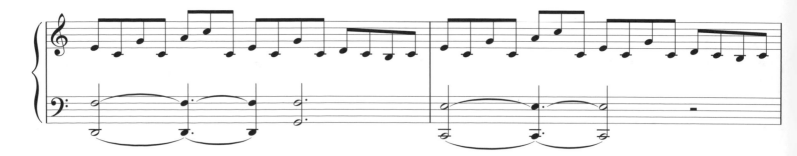

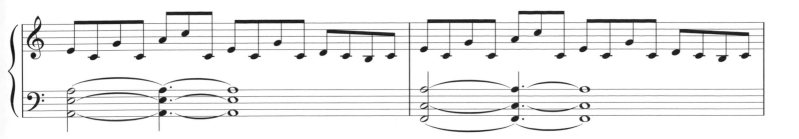

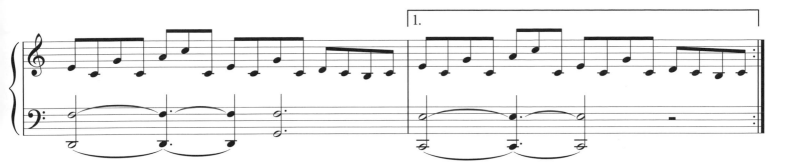

To Coda ⊕

D. % *(with repeat) al Coda*   ⊕ **CODA**

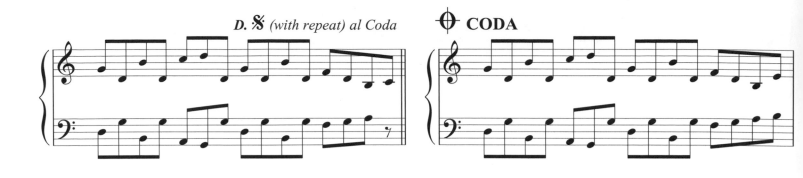

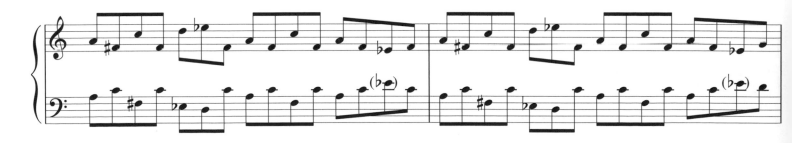

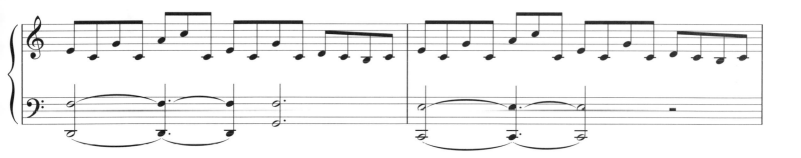

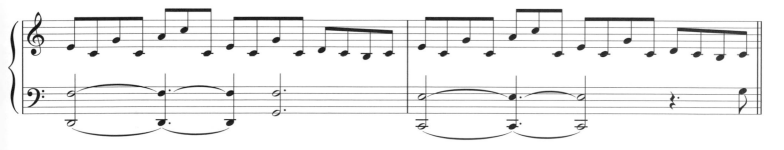

Play 11 times

jean de florette

(theme)

By Jean-Claude Petit

Moderately slow

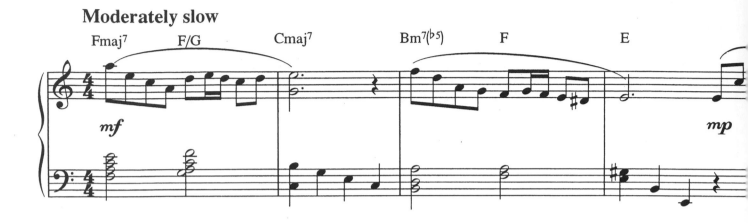

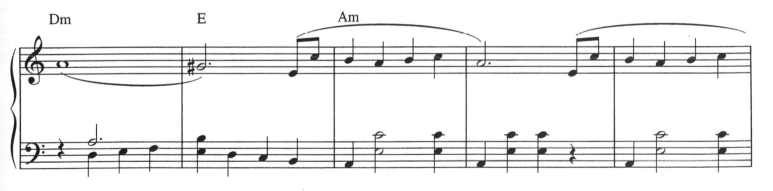

piano concerto no.5

in F minor
2nd Movement: Largo

By Johann Sebastian Bach

Largo ($\quad$ = c.56)

flower duet

from "lakmé"

By Leo Delibes
Arranged by Simon Lesley

Delicately (♪ = 112)

mp

very little pedal

'moonlight' sonata op.27 no.2
(adagio sostenuto)

By Ludwig van Beethoven

Adagio sostenuto

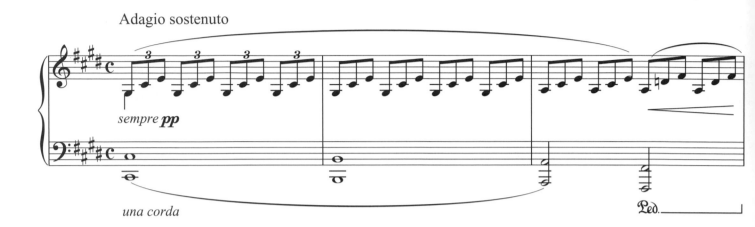

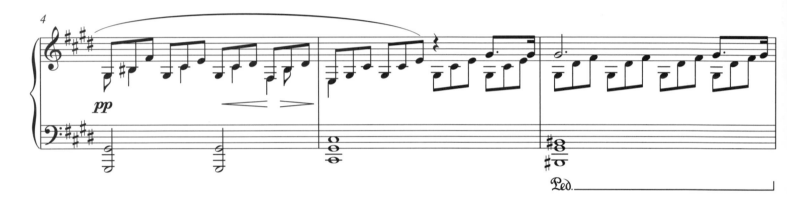

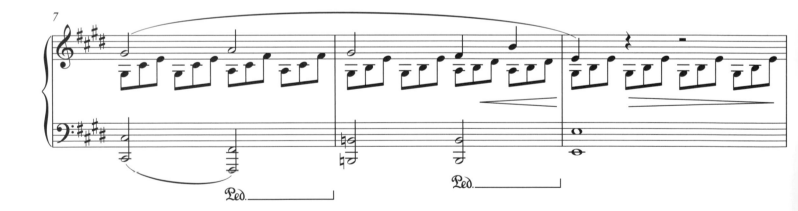

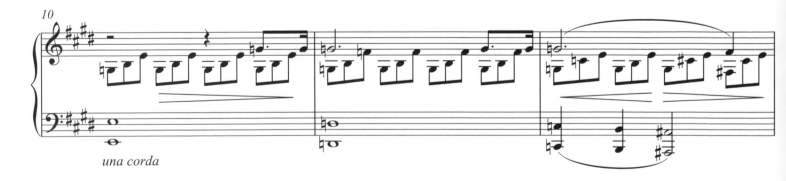

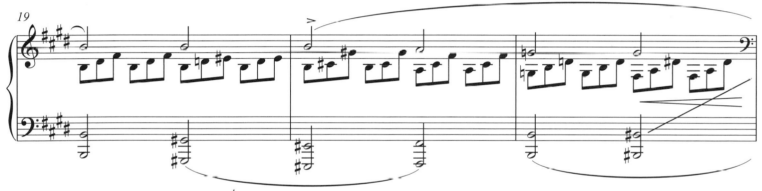

marcato, ma sempre **p**

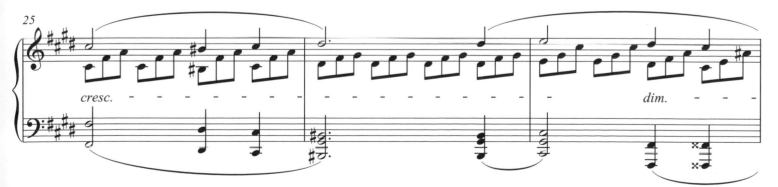

25

una corda

il basso sempre

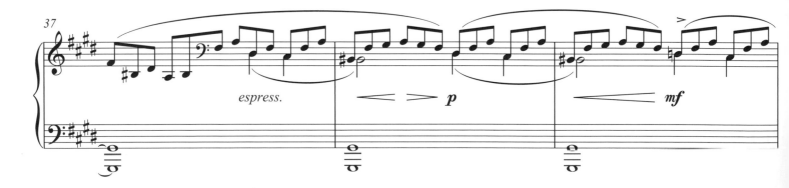

poco rit.   a tempo   più marcato del
                                                                                       principio

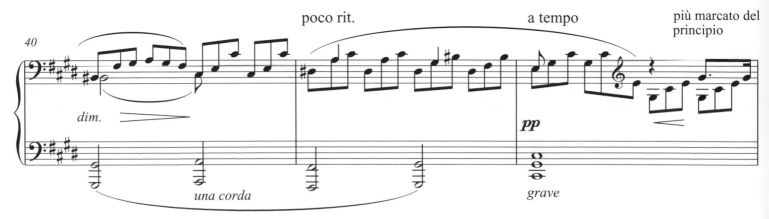

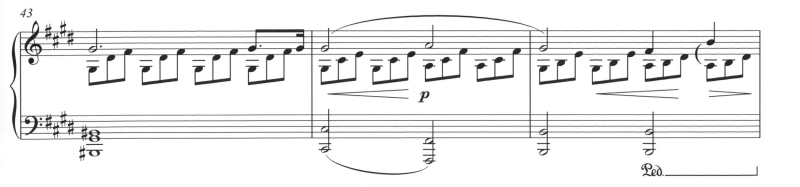

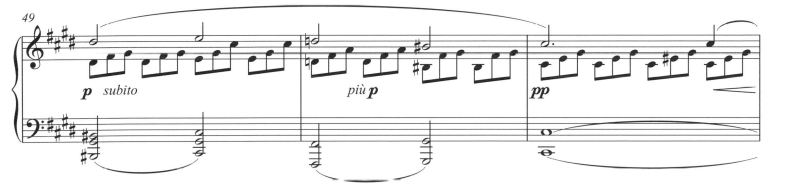

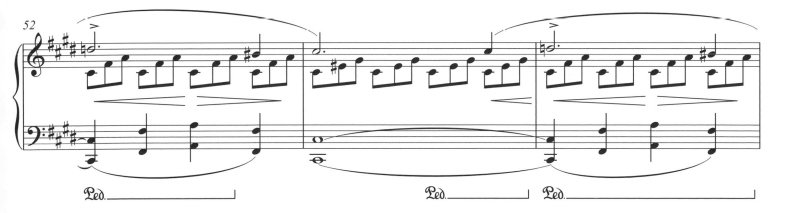

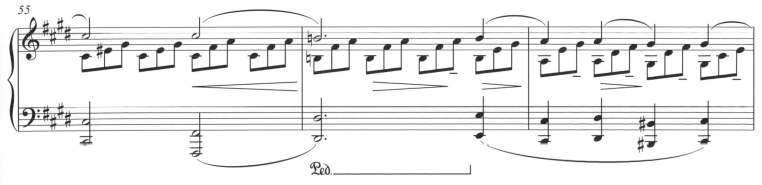

sempre legatissimo

una corda

slentando

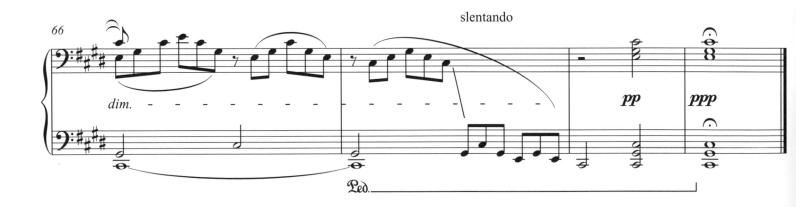

clair de lune
from "suite bergamasque"

By Claude Debussy
Arranged by Jack Long

Andante espressivo

Tempo rubato

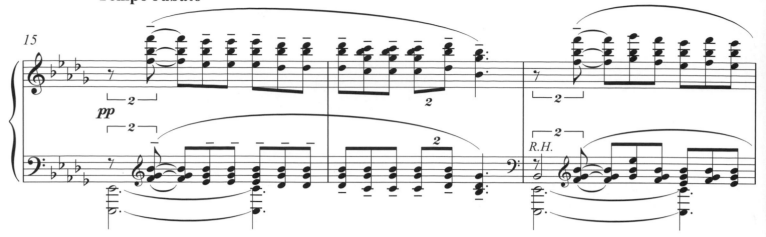

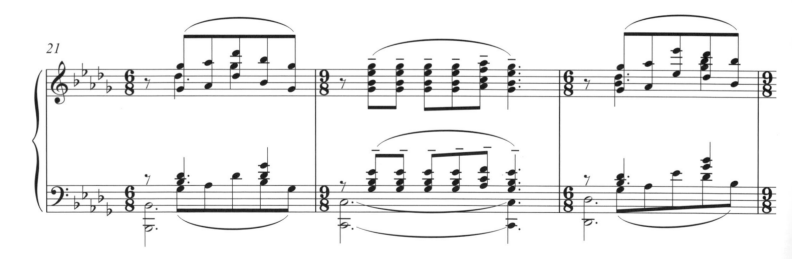

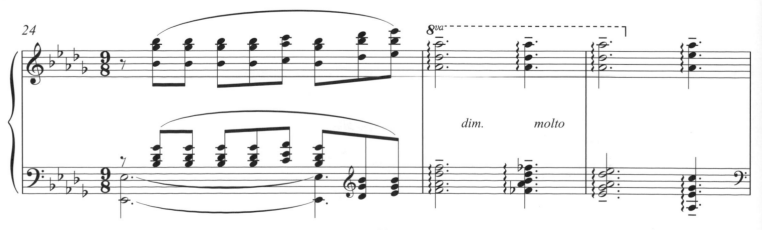

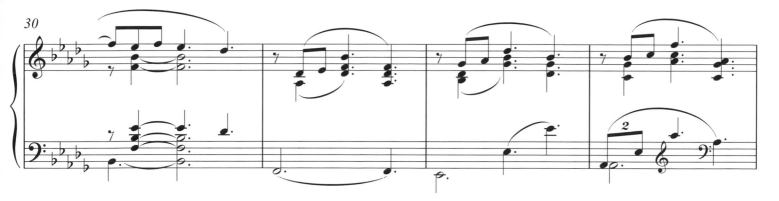

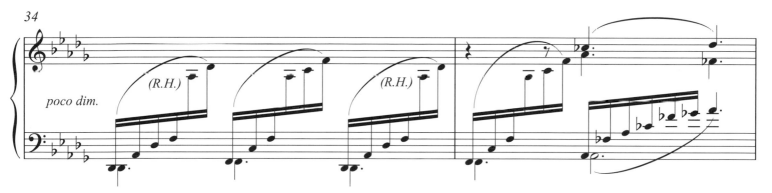

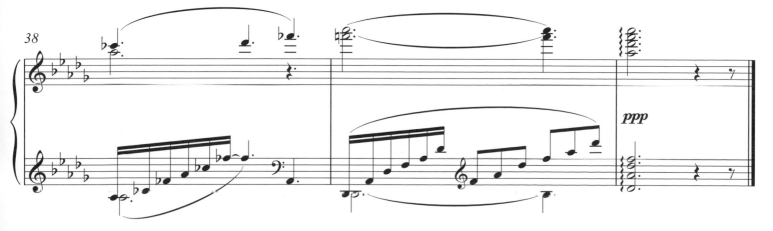

barcarolle
from "the tales of hoffmann"

By Jacques Offenbach

Moderato

sempre più dolce — *morendo*

ppp

una corda

33

gymnopédie no.1

By Erik Satie

Lent et douloureux

gnossienne no.1

By Erik Satie

Du bout de la pensée

Postulez en vous-même

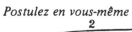

Pas à Pas

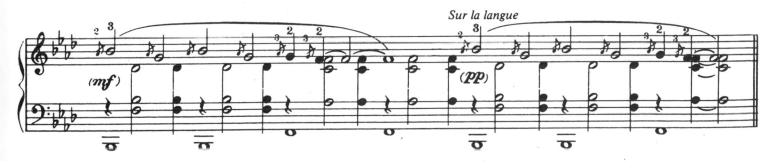

Sur la langue

weather storm

By Craig Armstrong, Robert Del Naja, Andrew Vowles, Grantley Marshall, Nellee Hooper,
Cedric Napoleon, James Lloyd, Curtis Harmon & Daniel Harmon
Arranged by Jack Long

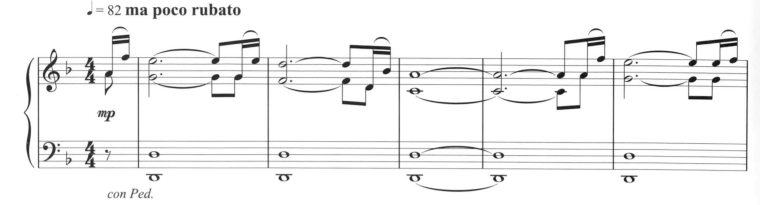

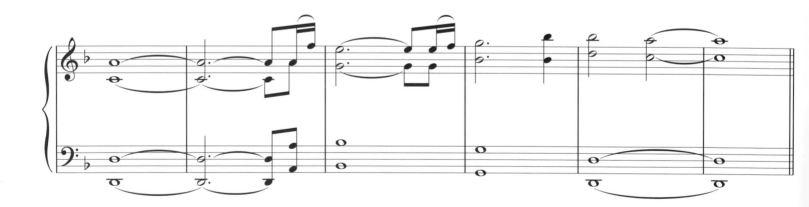

1 Quasi improvisato

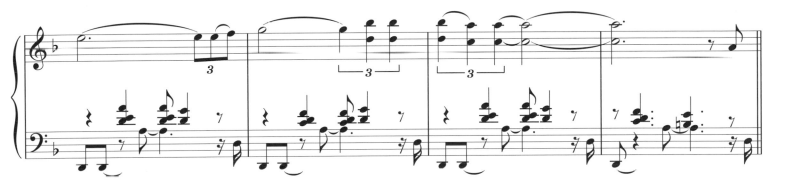

2

4 **Quasi improvisato**

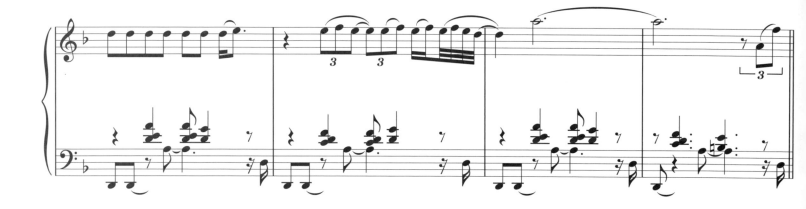

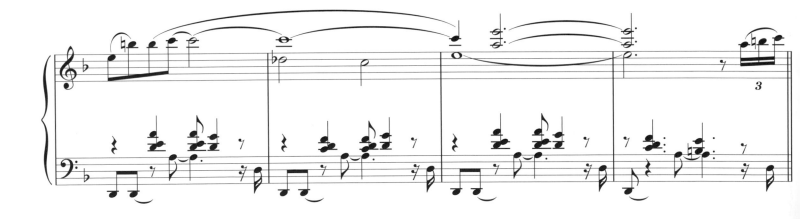

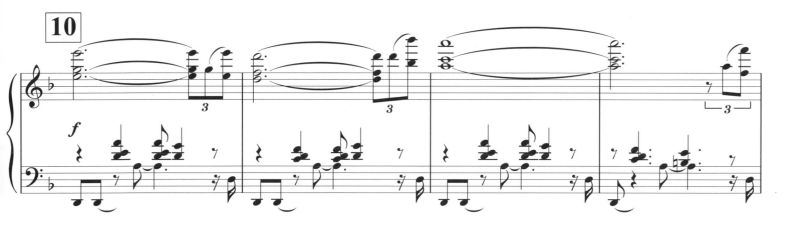

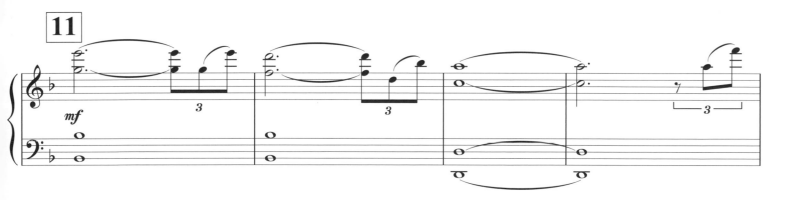

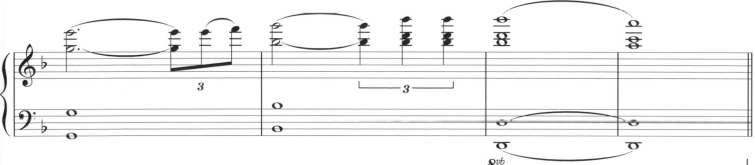

merry christmas, mr. lawrence

By Ryuichi Sakamoto
Arranged by Jack Long

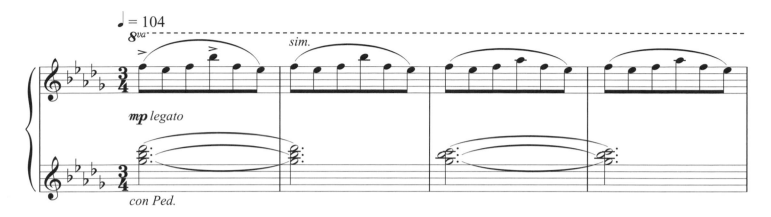

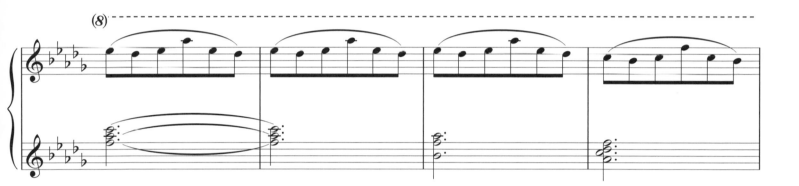

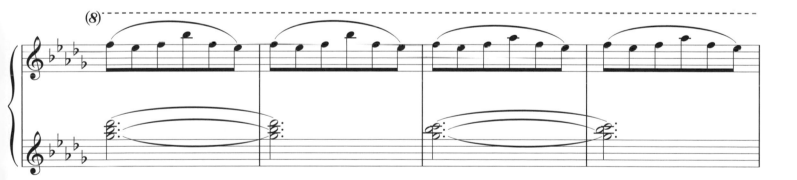

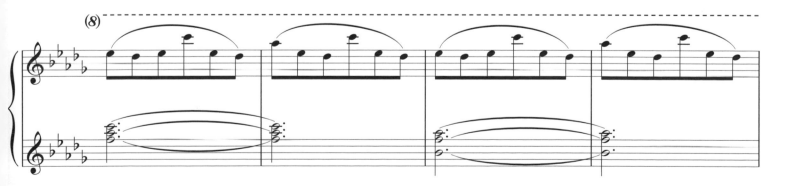

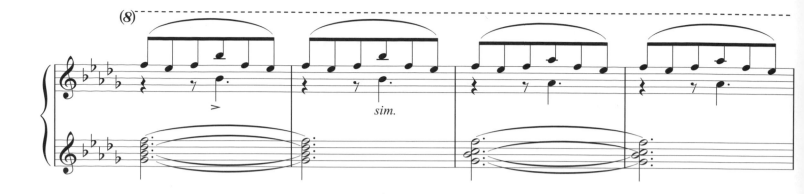

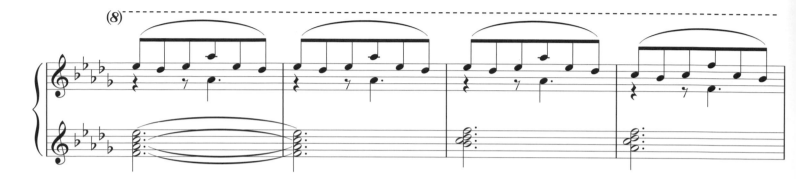

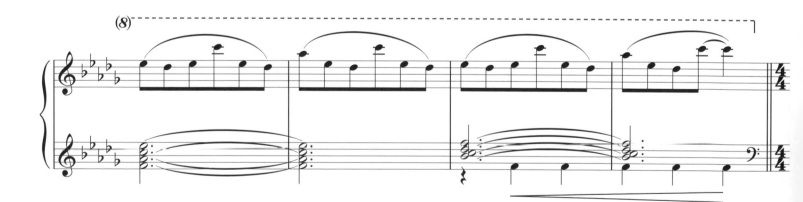

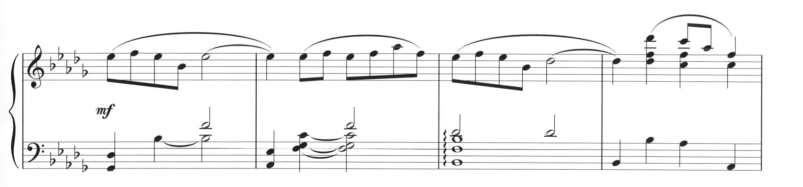

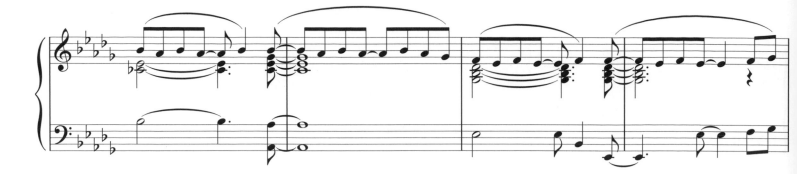

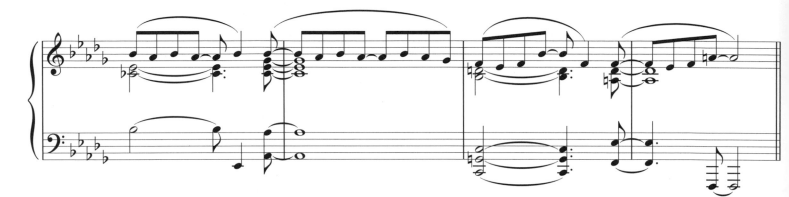

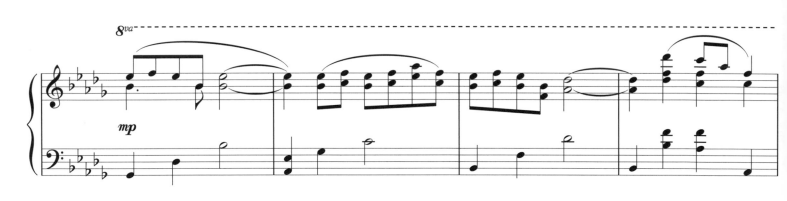

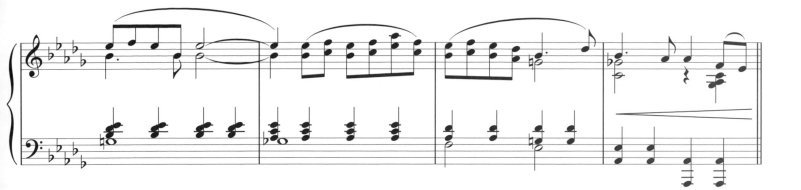

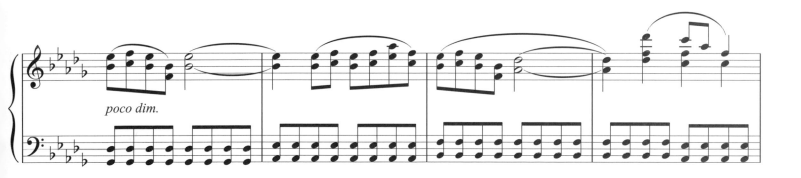

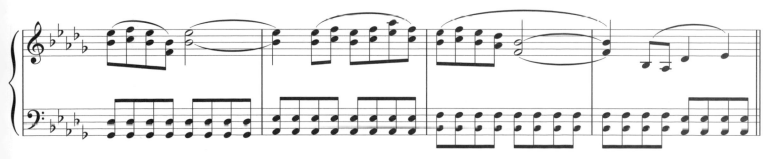

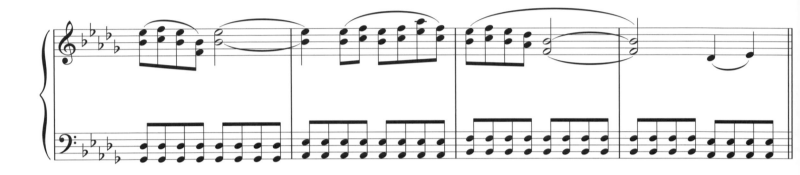

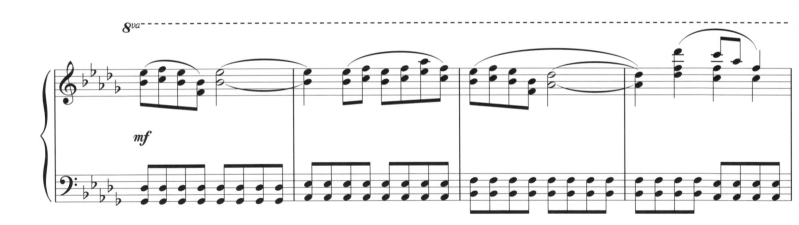

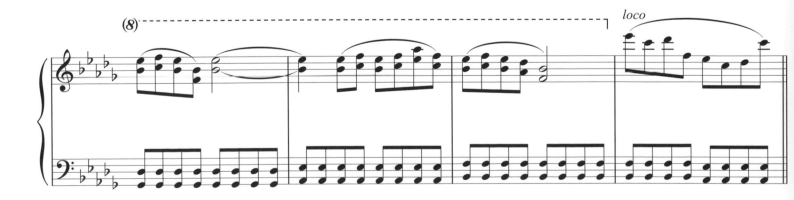

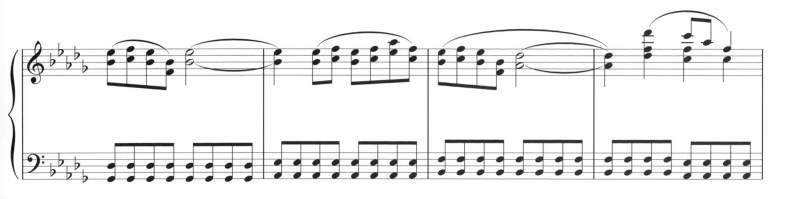

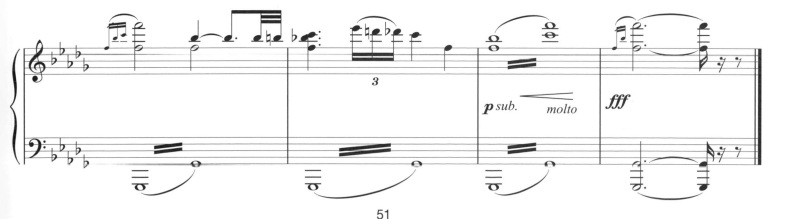

piano concerto no.1

in E minor (romance: larghetto)

By Frédéric Chopin
Arranged by Jerry Lanning

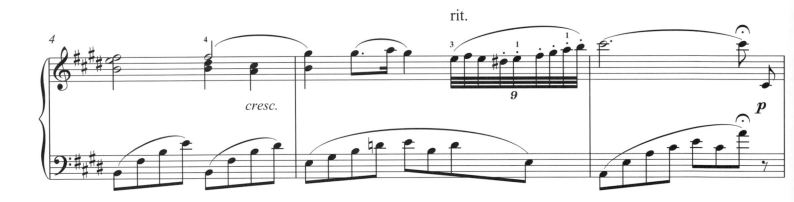

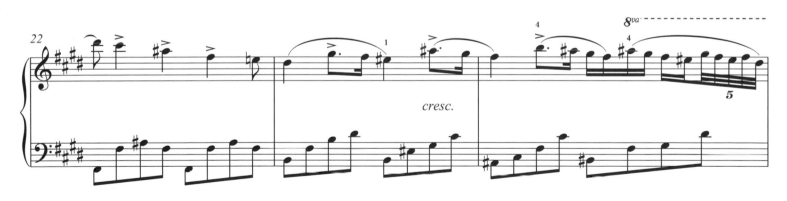

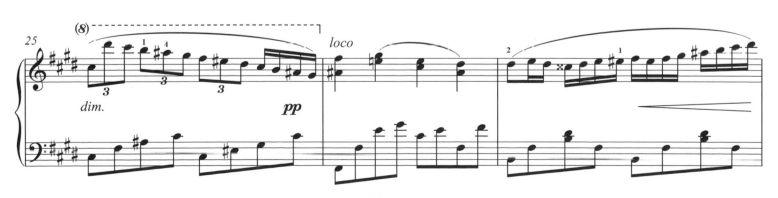

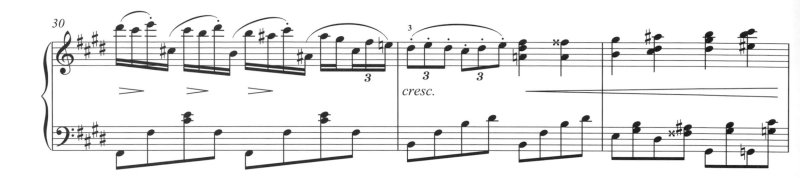

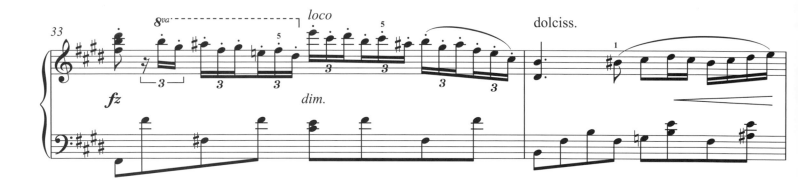

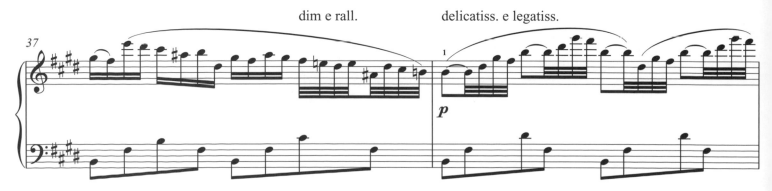

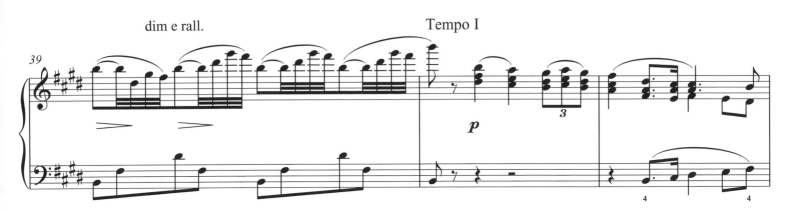

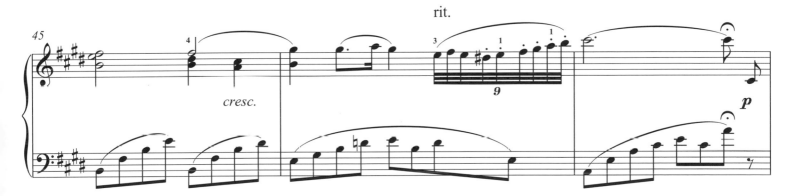

time to say goodbye
(con te partirò)

By Lucio Quarantotto & Francesco Sartori

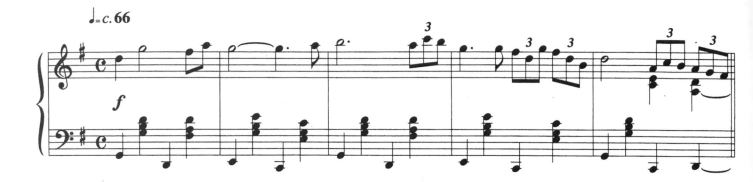

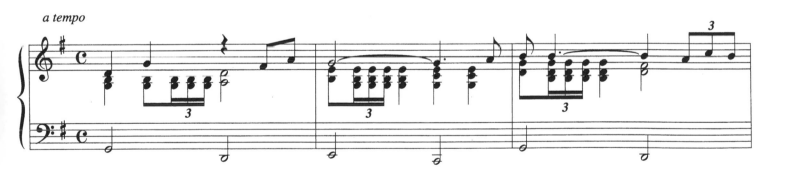

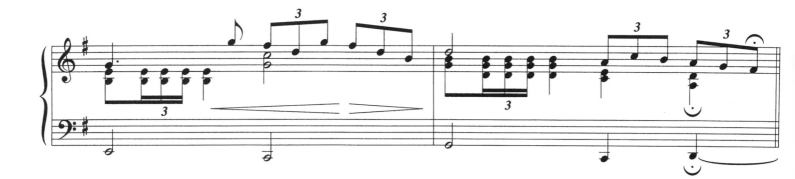

poco rit.

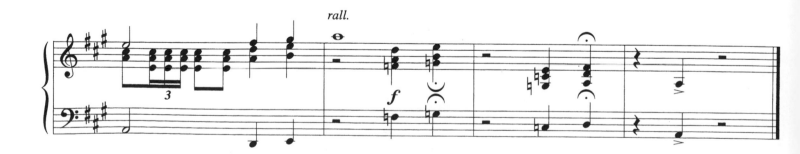

chi mai

(theme from the tv series "the life and times of david lloyd george")

By Ennio Morricone

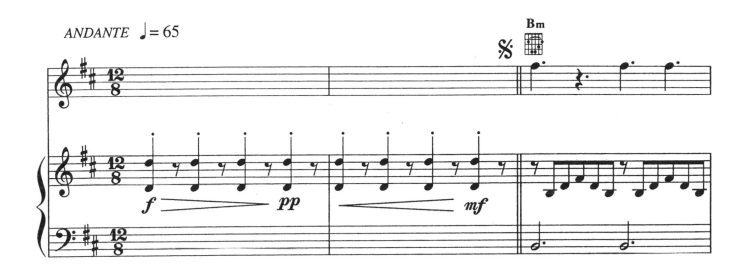

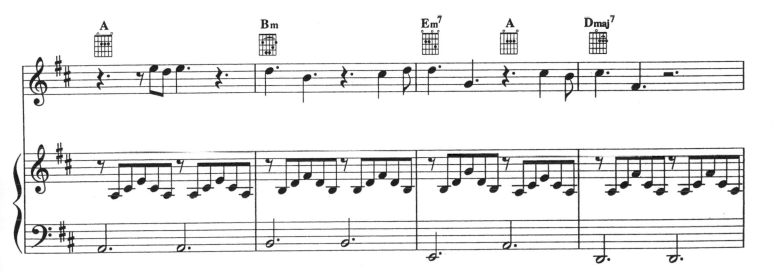

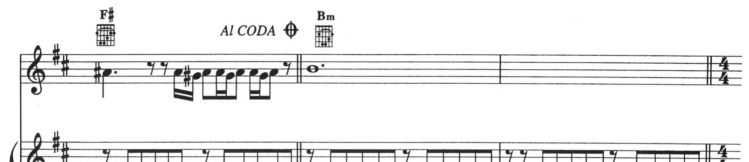

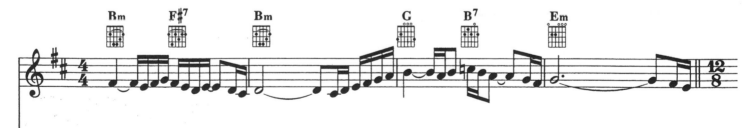

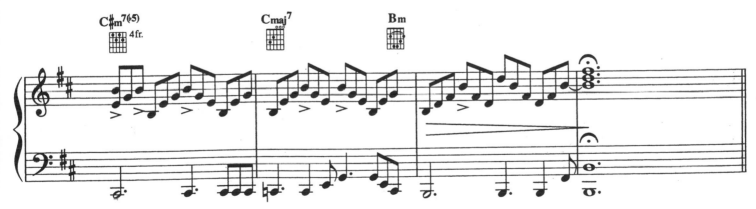

aria
from "goldberg variations"

By Johann Sebastian Bach

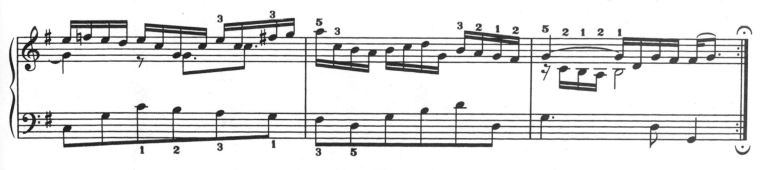

the heart asks pleasure first:
the promise/the sacrifice

(from "the piano")

By Michael Nyman

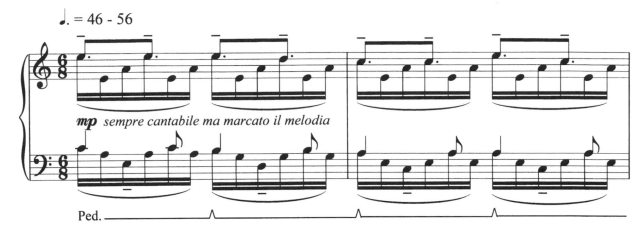

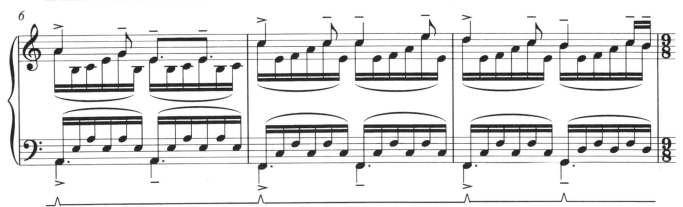

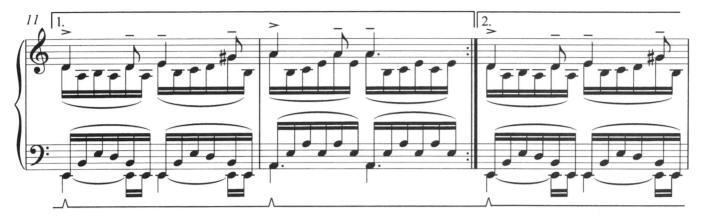

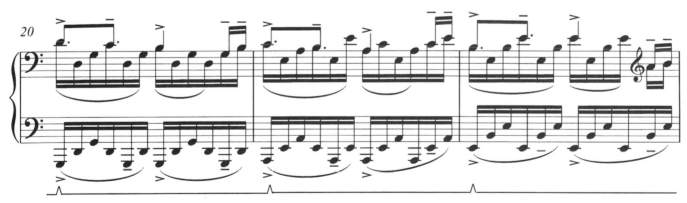

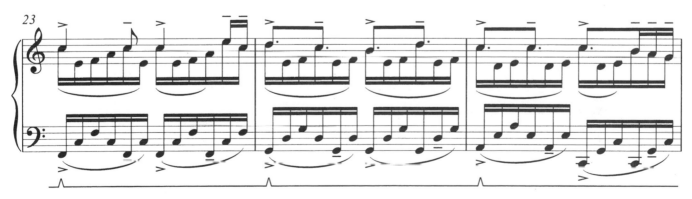

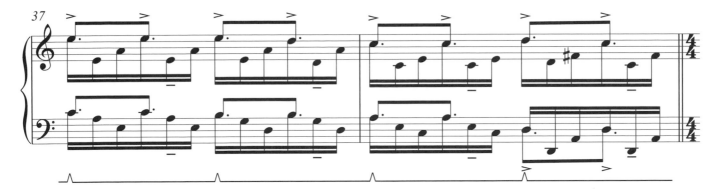

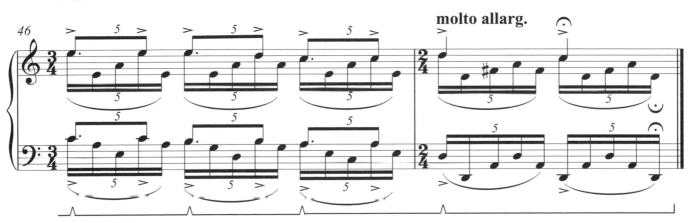

aquarium

from "the carnival of the animals"

By Camille Saint-Saëns

Andantino

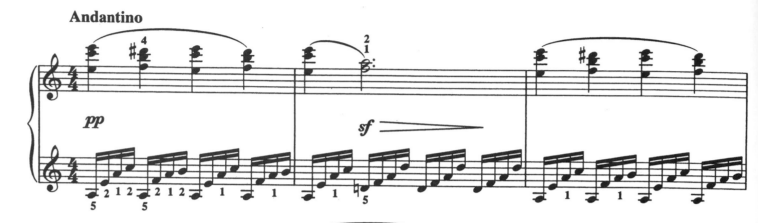

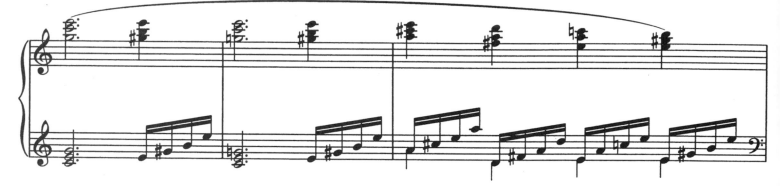

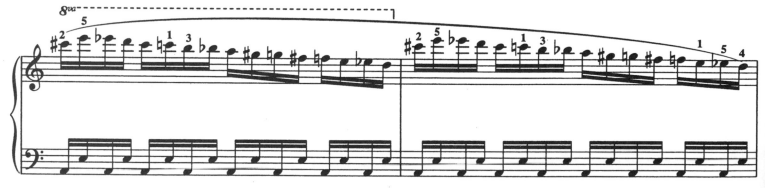

sheep may safely graze

By Johann Sebastian Bach

Gently moving

sarabande
in D minor

By George Frideric Handel

a tempo

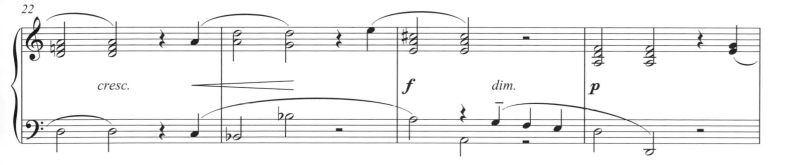

molto rit.

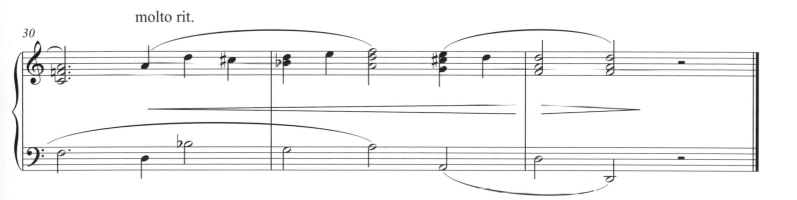

allegretto

from "symphony no.7 in A major" (2nd movement)
(Figlio Perduto)

By Ludwig van Beethoven
Arranged by Jack Long

Allegretto (♩ = 76)

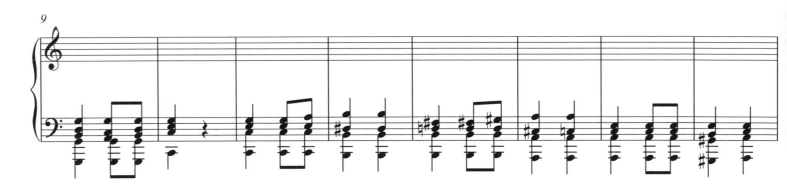

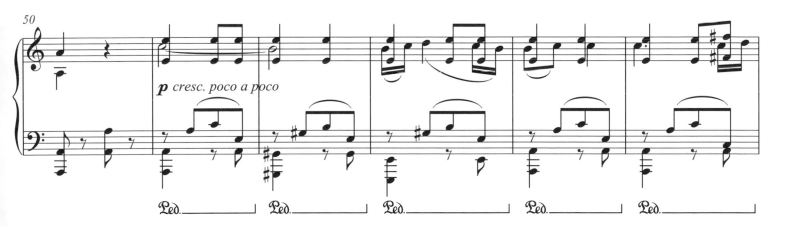

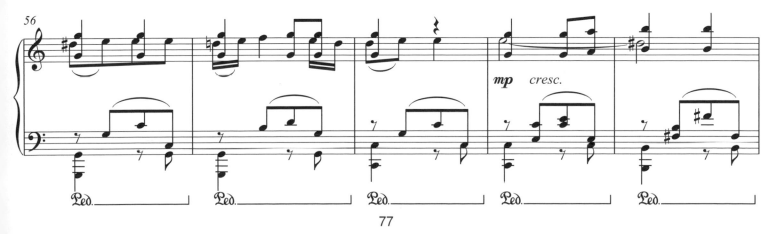

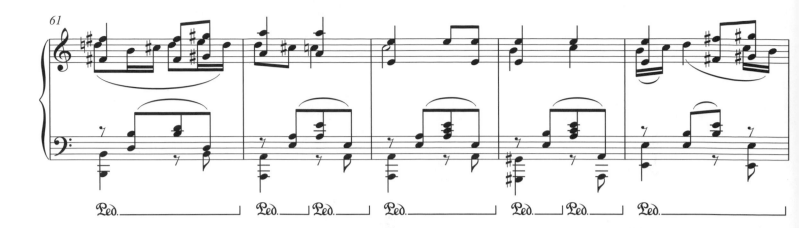

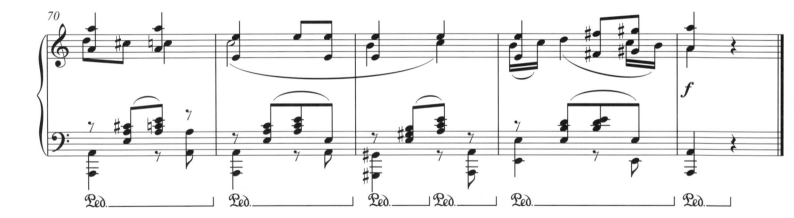

If you like this book you will also like these for solo piano

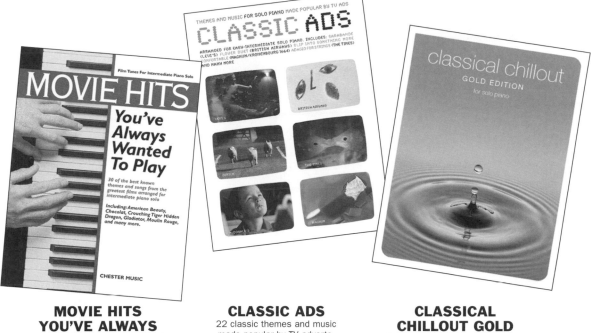

MOVIE HITS YOU'VE ALWAYS WANTED TO PLAY

30 of the best known themes and songs from the greatest films arranged for intermediate solo piano. Includes: *American Beauty, Chocolat, Crouching Tiger Hidden Dragon, Moulin Rouge!*, and many more.
Order No. CH65439

CLASSIC ADS

22 classic themes and music made popular by TV adverts. Includes: Adagio for Strings (The Times), 633 Squadron (Zurich), Johnny And Mary (Renault Clio), Fields Of Gold (Cancer Research).
Order No. CH65989

CLASSICAL CHILLOUT GOLD

Unwind with this great sequel to our best selling *classical chillout* containing 29 super cool piano favourites to play and enjoy. Includes: Adagio for Strings (Barber), The Lamb (Tavener) and Pavane (Fauré)
Order No. CH66319

THE GOLD SERIES

A beautifully presented series of albums containing the most famous masterpieces from the world's greatest composers.

MOZART GOLD

Includes: A Musical Joke, Piano Concerto No.21 'Elvira Madigan', Serenade in B♭ 'Gran Partita' and Symphony No.40 in G minor.
Order No. CH65505

BEETHOVEN GOLD

Includes: Symphony No.5, Für Elise, Minuet in G and the popular 'Moonlight' Sonata.
Order No. CH65670

CHOPIN GOLD

Includes: All famous waltzes, nocturnes, preludes and mazurkas as well as excerpts from Piano Concerto No.1, Ballade in G minor and Sonata No.2 in B♭ Minor.
Order No. CH65681

TCHAIKOVSKY GOLD

Includes: 1812 Overture, plus music from *The Nutcracker, Sleeping Beauty* and *Swan Lake*.
Order No. CH65692

For more information on these and the thousands of other titles available from Chester Music and Music Sales, please contact:

Music Sales Limited
*Newmarket Road, Bury St Edmunds, Suffolk, IP33 3YB.
Tel: 01284 702600. Fax: 01284 768301.
www.musicsales.com*

Bringing you the words and the music

All the latest music in print... rock & pop plus jazz, blues, country, classical and the best in West End show scores.

- Books to match your favourite CDs.

- Book-and-CD titles with high quality backing tracks for you to play along to. Now you can play guitar or piano with your favourite artist... or simply sing along!

- Audition songbooks with CD backing tracks for both male and female singers for all those with stars in their eyes.

- Can't read music? No problem, you can still play all the hits with our wide range chord songbooks.

- Check out our range of instrumental tutorial titles, taking you from novice to expert in no time at all!

- Musical show scores include *The Phantom Of The Opera*, *Les Misérables*, *Mamma Mia* and many more hit productions.

- DVD master classes featuring the techniques of top artists.